Rush, Rush, Rush

Written by Diane Engles
Illustrated by Mike Lester

Shut the door.

Then mop the floor.

Rush, rush, rush.

Take a bath.

Then do your math.

Rush, rush, rush.

Catch a fish.

Then wash a dish.

Rush, rush, rush.

Clean the shed.

Then make your bed.

Rush, rush, rush.

There's no time to do much more.

Grandmother is at the door.